DREAM BIG

Know What You Want, Why You Want It,
and What You're Going to Do About It

STUDY GUIDE | FIVE SESSIONS

BOB GOFF

NELSON
BOOKS

An Imprint of Thomas Nelson

Published in Nashville, Tennessee, by Nelson Books. Nelson Books and Thomas Nelson are registered trademarks of HarperCollins Christian Publishing, Inc.

All Scripture quotations are taken from *The Holy Bible, New International Version*®, NIV®. Copyright © 1973, 1978, 1984, 2011 by Biblica, Inc.™ Used by permission. All rights reserved worldwide.

Thomas Nelson titles may be purchased in bulk for educational, business, fundraising, or sales promotional use. For information, please e-mail SpecialMarkets@ThomasNelson.com.

ISBN 978-0-310-12132-9 (softcover)
ISBN 978-0-310-12133-6 (ebook)

First Printing March 2020 / Printed in the United States of America

CONTENTS

INTRODUCTION

You become fully awake to your biggest and
most worthwhile ambitions by becoming fully awake
to yourself and your God-given purpose.

BOB GOFF

WELCOME TO *DREAM BIG!*

All of us have ambitions and long to do more in this life. But
we also have all kinds of distractions, misunderstandings,
and assumptions blurring what we need to do to bring our
dreams to life. In order to tap into our deepest passions and
unleash the purpose God has for us, we must assess our
understanding of who we are and how God sees us. We must
sort through the messages we have been given and find our
truest ambitions. This includes looking at disappointing
areas of our lives as well as those we perceive as failures.

This process won't be easy. But the good news is that you
won't do it alone. This group is the ideal place to dig deeper
and uncover the big dreams inside you—the ones you dared

to pursue before others told you it was impossible or irrational to chase them. God has a wild and exciting dream for your life, and it is time to take the necessary steps to see it clearly and make it reality. Not only will you confront your deepest desires with clarity, but you will also identify the obstacles holding you back so you can come up with a plan to overcome them. You can reconnect with your passions and be the big dreamer God made you to be.

Here is how it works. *Dream Big* is a five-session study in exploring your hopes, dreams, ambitions, and the real purpose God has implanted within you. Each session will explore a different aspect of what it means to dream big through the teachings Bob Goff. There will be an opening question, a brief Bible reading, and then you will watch Bob on the video.

The good stuff, however, comes after the video, when you dig deeper into each topic in a guided small-group time. This makes space to process the message and get practical about what it means in your life. You will discuss your responses, ask questions, and hear more about the dreams that God is revealing in the lives of others.

So, are you ready? Then it's time to rediscover how to *dream big.*

HOW TO USE THIS GUIDE

As you will discover throughout this study, dreaming big is practical. It requires you to take chances and do things. Dreams require reflection but also risk-taking. This study is designed to give you opportunities for both.

Each session begins with an icebreaker type question followed by a reflection from the Bible. Then you will watch Bob's teaching on the video before diving into some directed discussion with your group. Even though there are many questions provided to facilitate your group discussion, don't feel like you have to use them all. Your leader will focus on the ones that resonate with your group and guide you from there.

The final section of each session (called "Dream") is where this study might diverge from others you have done, as you and your small group will engage in practical exercises to bring home the teaching to you. These exercises are designed to be completed during your meeting, and they will be as worthwhile as you make them. If you choose to only go through the motions or resist participating, you will find them less than satisfying. But if you give them a try, you may discover that they will help you to rediscover your dreams and make them come alive.

At the end of each session, there are more opportunities for you to engage with the content during the week through the personal studies. These studies include activities to help you reflect on what you're learning, explore a passage from the Bible, and help you to put your dreams into action. You are invited to do at least one of these activities between sessions and to use this study guide to record what you learned.

Beginning in session two, there will be time before the video teaching to check in, share the previous week's activity, and process your experiences as a group. If you're unable to complete the between-sessions exercises or are new to the group, don't worry. Hearing what others have learned will be nourishment enough.

Remember that all this is an opportunity to explore new ways of considering what it means to *dream big*. The videos, discussions, and exercises are all intended to kick-start your imagination so you will be inspired to try things on your own. Just imagine what God could do with a whole group of people who are passionate about owning their dreams and making them reality. Let's jump into *Dream Big* and find out.

Note: *If you are a group leader, there are additional instructions and resources in the back of this guide to help you lead your members through the study. Because some of the activities require materials and setup, make sure you read this over ahead of time so you will be prepared.*

GET READY TO DREAM BIG

There is a path to discover and release your
most beautiful and lasting ambitions into the world.

BOB GOFF

WELCOME

Once upon a time, as kids or young adults, we had big dreams.
Now life has become a maze of responsibilities, obligations,
expectations, and assumptions about who we are and what
we must do. We know there must be more to life than we are
experiencing. Maybe we sense something deep inside stirring
us occasionally before we are distracted by the next crisis or
urgent diversion. We may even believe God put us where we
are for a purpose . . . but that purpose seems out of reach. We
still have dreams, but we are no longer in touch with them.

No matter where you are, know that it's not too late for
you to still dream big. This study is designed to help you
realize your deepest longing and your purpose by peeling
away the layers of distracting buildup that have prevented
you from actualizing your dreams. Layers of messages—
sometimes contradictory—from family and friends, teachers

and pastors, coaches and bosses, neighbors and acquaintances about who you should be and how you should act.

God didn't create you to be defined by these layers of messages from the other people in your life! He made you unique in his own image so that you could bring your dreams to life.

SHARE

To get started, take a few minutes to introduce yourself to anyone you do not know in the group. Then jump into the theme of this session by discussing the following questions:

- One dream I've had since childhood is _____ _____ .

- Sharing it right now with the group, I feel _____ _____ because _____ .

READ

Invite someone to read aloud the following passage. Listen for new insights as you hear the verses being read and then discuss the questions that follow.

Jesus went up to Jerusalem for one of the Jewish festivals. Now there is in Jerusalem near the Sheep Gate a pool, which in Aramaic is called Bethesda and which is surrounded by five covered colonnades. Here a great number of disabled people used to lie—the blind, the lame, the paralyzed. From time to time an angel of the Lord would come down and stir up the waters. The first one into the pool after each such disturbance would be cured of whatever disease they had.

One who was there had been an invalid for thirty-eight years. When Jesus saw him lying there and learned that he had been in this condition for a long time, he asked him, "Do you want to get well?"

"Sir," the invalid replied, "I have no one to help me into the pool when the water is stirred. While I am trying to get in, someone else goes down ahead of me."

Then Jesus said to him, "Get up! Pick up your mat and walk." At once the man was cured; he picked up his mat and walked (John 5:1-9).

Why do you think Jesus asked the blind man, "Do you want to get well," before healing him? While it may seem obvious that the man is there beside the pool hoping for his sight to be restored, why did Jesus consider it important to ask the man what he wanted?

Have you ever seen someone pursuing a goal for a long time only to lose sight of what he or she really wanted? What were the circumstances?

WATCH

Play the video segment for session one. As you watch, use the following outline to record any questions you have or points that stand out to you.

It's important to go deeper if you want to explore the big dreams God has for you.

In order to dream big, you need clarity—and the way to see more clearly is to be authentic about who you are, where you are, and what you want.

Looking at your past mistakes, disappointments, and failures will often reveal vital clues about your life's purpose.

Remembering that you are God's beloved child is the key to your true identity.

Being real about where you are in life isn't easy, but it's important in order for you to know what you want so you can dream big.

Stop merely waving at your dreams and ambitions and choose to follow them.

If you want to uncover your dreams, you need to give Jesus free rein in your life and not just a few areas here and there.

Whatever moves you from thinking about what *needs* to be done to actually *doing* it often reveals something important about your lifelong ambitions.

DISCUSS

Take a few minutes to discuss what you just watched and explore these concepts with your group.

1. Jesus told the disciples to "push out a little deeper" after fishing all night but catching nothing. What does it look like for you to "push out a little deeper" to dream big? What typically prevents you from going deeper—with yourself and with others?

2. What obstacles have blocked you from pursuing your dreams? How have you handled those barriers? How have those setbacks blurred the way that you now see your ambitions?

3. What in your past continues to hinder you from dreaming big in the present? What do these hindrances reveal about your dreams? About the way you've pursued them?

4. When an acquaintance asks *who* you are, how do you usually respond? If you take out your titles, positions, or status at work (manager, sales rep, vice president), as well as your roles (spouse, parent, caretaker, sibling, friend, neighbor), what is left? How do you think of yourself apart from your responsibilities and relationships?

5. What pops into your mind when you consider *where* you are in life right now? If you were someone else looking at your life and trying to be objective, how would you answer this question? Where are you in this season of life? In the group tonight?

6. Do you agree that knowing *who you are* and *where you are* basically reveals *what you want*? Why or why not? What dreams do you want to pursue right now?

DREAM

(For this activity, you will need a sheet of paper and a pen or pencil. Markers, colored pencils, crayons, and art supplies are optional but would be a great addition if they are available.)

If you want to get to a place you haven't visited before, it's always helpful to consult a map. Whether digital or hard copies, maps identify your starting location and provide you with directions to a destination. A simple "you are here" notation on a map at a theme part, a museum, or trailhead can provide a foundation for you to get your bearings. Maps also provide a visual illustration of what is between your starting point and where you want to end up. Maps help you choose the shortest routes or circumvent roadblocks and dead ends. Having a map can provide clarity about what you need in order to get where you are going.

With this in mind, grab a sheet of paper and take a few minutes to create a map with your big dreams as your destination. It can look like any version of a map you want—the goal is simply to draw, sketch, or doodle a map that indicates *where you are* currently and *where you want to go* over the course of the next few years. Include any speed bumps and detours, including the ones you already know as well as ones you anticipate. Remember there is no right or wrong way to do this and no extra points for being creative or artistic. Just have fun as you create this visual depiction of getting from where you are to where your big dreams come alive.

After you come up with your map, share with the group. Tell the other mapmakers something you notice about their maps and what it reveals about them, about their view of God, about their dreams, or about what they must overcome to reach their dreams. After everyone has had a turn, hang on to your map as a reference for future activities.

CLOSE

Close the meeting by praying together and asking God's blessing on all that has been shared. Ask him to provide clarity as you go deeper and consider where you are and where you want to go. Let the Holy Spirit be the compass that ultimately helps you navigate your dream map.

BETWEEN-SESSIONS PERSONAL STUDY

If you have not already started reading *Dream Big,* now is a great time to begin. This week, you may want to review chapters 1–13 in the book (the chapters are short) before engaging in the following between-session activities. Be sure to read the reflection questions after each activity and make a few notes in your guide about the experience. There will be a few minutes for you to share any insights you learned at the start of the next session.

REFLECT: DARE TO DREAM

Take a few minutes to reflect on the following questions and record your answers:

> What were your dreams when you were a child? What kind of life did you imagine for yourself? What did you long for the most?

Which of your childhood dreams have stayed with you? Which ones have you totally abandoned? Why?

What obstacles have you faced in trying to dream big? What setbacks and barriers have you overcome so far?

How has your sense of purpose in life shaped your dreams? How has it shaped the way you are currently pursuing your dreams?

What is the difference between "sleepwalking" and "sitting still" as you consider pursuing your dreams? How has God been "waking you up" lately?

Which ambitions have you pursued only to discover they belonged to someone else—your parents, teachers, coaches, or friends? Are you still chasing something that is not part of your big dream? What do you need to let go of in order to be available to God?

READ: **KEEP FISHING**

Read the following passage found in Luke 5:1–11:

One day as Jesus was standing by the Lake of Gennesaret, the people were crowding around him and listening to the word of God. He saw at the water's edge two boats, left there by the fishermen, who were washing their nets. He got into one of the boats, the one belonging to Simon, and asked him to put out a little from shore. Then he sat down and taught the people from the boat.

When he had finished speaking, he said to Simon, "Put out into deep water, and let down the nets for a catch."

Simon answered, "Master, we've worked hard all night and haven't caught anything. But because you say so, I will let down the nets."

When they had done so, they caught such a large number of fish that their nets began to break. So they signaled their partners in the other boat to come and help them, and they came and filled both boats so full that they began to sink.

When Simon Peter saw this, he fell at Jesus' knees and said, "Go away from me, Lord; I am a sinful man!" For he and all his companions were astonished at the catch of fish they had taken, and so were James and John, the sons of Zebedee, Simon's partners.

Then Jesus said to Simon, "Don't be afraid; from now on you will fish for people." So they pulled their boats up on shore, left everything and followed him.

It must have seemed strange to these fishermen when a stranger showed up, hopped in one of their boats, taught the Word of God, and then told them to put out into deeper water. To Simon's credit, after expressing his initial skepticism, he agreed to follow what the stranger said—simply because he had directed to do so. The results exceeded anything the fishermen could have imagined as their catch burst their nets and sank their boats! After fishing all night and catching nothing, the men had risked casting their nets just a little farther out, just a little deeper, and—bam!—they had more fish than ever before.

All too often, we are like these disciples. We put in years of hard work, sleepless nights, and bait our hooks again and again . . . but continually come up empty. We wonder why we should keep going—why we should keep doing what God has instructed us to do when we can see no tangible results for all our efforts. But then push out in faith just one more time . . . and find a catch beyond our wildest dreams!

There is no doubt that we must do our part if we want to realize our dreams. We won't make our dreams come to life by sitting around and only thinking about them. Flying requires wings and—as the Wright brothers discovered—

sometimes you have to keep tweaking them until they are just right. You change the angle, try a lighter wood, alter the wingspan. Then you catch the wind . . . and next thing you know, you're airborne!

Why do you think Jesus finished teaching before telling Simon to try again in deeper waters? If you had been in Simon's place, how would you have responded?

What role has faith played in the formation and pursuit of your dreams? When have you taken a risk or made a leap of faith and discovered more than you expected?

What does obeying God in faith have to do with making your dreams come alive? Why is it impossible to birth your biggest ambitions *without* following God's lead?

What risk is God calling you to make right now as you consider old dreams and new possibilities? What have you sidelined or given up on that you need to try again?

ACT: COLLECT PIECES OF YOUR PUZZLE

While none of us enjoy looking at our biggest failures, they can provide vital clues to help us recognize our dreams, ambitions, and deepest longings. Our mistakes, disappointments, and losses are important pieces of our "dream puzzle," and looking at them can illustrate our dreams in new ways and reveal areas in which some pieces fit and others do not. Today, use the following questions to collect and analyze some of your life's puzzle pieces.

WINS

List five examples of times you have reached a goal, achieved a milestone, won an award, earned a promotion, or been recognized for something you are good at doing.

Which of these do you consider your greatest achievement in life? Why?

Which of these do others usually consider your greatest achievement? If these are different than your choice, what do you think accounts for the difference?

What goal, pursuit, ambition, or dream is not on this list but remains alive in your heart?

LOSSES

List five examples of times when you have failed to reach a goal or complete something important you started, made a crucial error in judgment, suffered a loss you didn't see coming, or endured a disappointment that you think you could have prevented.

Which one of these has caused the greatest consequences or the most collateral damage in your life? Do you consider this your life's greatest failure? Why or why not?

If someone else looked at your list of losses, which item would they choose as the most painful setback or biggest failure? If these are different than your choice, what do you think accounts for the difference?

What mistake, failure, or loss is not on your list but nonetheless one you worry about? How has this prevented you from taking risks and dreaming big?

REFLECT

Take a minute to reflect on how you felt as you wrote each of these items on your "wins" and "losses" lists. How did you feel as you thought about your life's greatest wins and losses? Why do you think you felt this way?

What did you notice that surprised you the most? What dream-big clue, direction, or indicator can you take away from this exercise?

For Next Week: Use the space below to write any other key insights or questions from your personal study that you want to discuss at the next group meeting. In preparation for next week, review chapters 14–18 in *Dream Big.*

SET ABSURD EXPECTATIONS

*Want ambitions that want you back,
because that's where there's an opportunity.*

BOB GOFF

WELCOME

It can be so tempting to talk yourself out of dreaming big. This only makes it that much harder to burst through the walls of the box you build around your expectations and go for what seems impossible. However, when you dream big, it's important to imagine doing things that defy logic, common sense, or other people's expectations.

It's much easier to look at the distance between where you are *right now* and where your dreams would *require you to go*. But too often, considering the necessary details, steps, elements, and ingredients that must align for your ambitions to be realized only serves to reinforce the crazy-improbable odds against you. After all, if you think your journey is too long to arrive at such a far-off destination, it will be difficult to take even the first step.

But dreaming big requires you to suspend your practical way of seeing things long enough to look beyond logistics and limitations. What if you *did* have enough time? What if a benefactor, investor, or venture capitalist *did* provide the funding? What if you *did* have the resources you think you need to make your big dreams an even bigger reality?

If you want your dreams to fly . . . you have to look to the sky! If you focus only on all the reasons you're likely to fail, you will keep your passion—along with your imagination, faith, and action—grounded. Sometimes, the key to dreaming big is setting absurd expectations, taking an honest look at your motivations, and then stepping out in faith.

SHARE

If you or any of your group members are meeting for the first time, take a few minutes to introduce yourselves. Then jump into the theme of this session by discussing the following:

- One goal that seems impossible right now is _____ _____ .

- One thing that stood out to me in my between-sessions studies that I would like to share with the group is _____ .

READ

Invite someone to read aloud the following passage. Listen for new insights as you hear the verses being read and then discuss the questions that follow.

Do not store up for yourselves treasures on earth, where moths and vermin destroy, and where thieves break in and steal. But store up for yourselves treasures in heaven, where moths and vermin do not destroy, and where thieves do not break in and steal. For where your treasure is, there your heart will be also. . . .

No one can serve two masters. Either you will hate the one and love the other, or you will be devoted to the one and despise the other. You cannot serve both God and money.

Therefore I tell you, do not worry about your life, what you will eat or drink; or about your body, what you will wear. Is not life more than food, and the body more than clothes? Look at the birds of the air; they do not sow or reap or store away in barns, and yet your heavenly Father feeds them. Are you not much more valuable than they? Can any one of you by worrying add a single hour to your life? . . .

But seek first his kingdom and his righteousness, and all these things will be given to you as well (Matthew 6:19–21, 24–27, 33).

What do you think Jesus means when he says to "store up treasures in heaven"? Why does he contrast storing up earthly treasures with investing in heavenly ones?

Where is most of your treasure (time, energy, attention, money) currently being invested? How does this align with what's most important in your life?

WATCH

Play the video segment for session two. As you watch, use the following outline to record any questions you have or points that stand out to you.

It's easy to undermine the pursuit of your dreams by assuming they are unattainable. Instead, begin by removing all filters and listing all ambitions, dreams, and goals that come to mind.

Take your list of big dreams and examine your motivation for pursuing each one. Then vet each item through the lens of Scripture. Are these ambitions ones that Jesus said would outlast you?

Evaluate your ambitions by comparing them to one another. Rank them based on your passion for each one, the cost in resources (time, energy, money, focus), and the bigger cause that is served.

God delights when you take a step toward him in pursuit of the purpose he has given you.

Think about the impact your dreams will have on any and all people involved—including your family and loved ones.

Look for opportunities to take your ambitions for a test drive to get better acquainted.

DISCUSS

Take a few minutes to discuss what you just watched and explore these concepts with your group.

1. What's the most off-the-wall dream you've been harboring? What inspired this dream or served as a catalyst in your imagination? What scares you most about pursuing it?

2. What are some of the dreams or goals you pursued when you were younger that now seem small or even selfish as you look back? What did attaining them (or not) teach you about yourself? What did it teach you about what matters the most to you?

3. How have your dreams and ambitions changed over the past few years? What has caused the change? How has your faith shaped these changes?

4. When have you experienced God's pleasure as you've pursued one of your dreams? What have experiences like this one shown you about your God-given purpose? How did this experience help you understand what it means to store up treasures in heaven?

5. How do most people you love respond to your dreams? Overall, have they helped you or hindered you in pursuit of your ambitions? How has their response—or what you assume their response will be—influenced your dream-related decisions?

6. When was the last time you researched or explored an area directly related to one of your big dreams? What were your findings? Did this experience increase your passion to pursue this dream or dampen your enthusiasm? Why or why not?

DREAM

(For this activity, you will need a sheet of paper and a pen or pencil.)

On a separate piece of paper, write down one big dream you would like to share with the rest of the group for vetting. In a couple of sentences, describe your connection or level of passion for this dream as well as your biggest obstacle, greatest fear, or critical expectation. Next, based on what you just wrote, share your dream as if pitching it to investors, supporters, and/or stakeholders. The rest of the group should listen carefully and then choose one of the following sets of questions to help you evaluate this dream, clarify your vision, and specify your next step:

- Is this dream meaningful and worthwhile? What enduring benefit will it provide to you?
- Is this dream all about you? How does it serve others? What impact will this dream have on other people? How will it help them?
- Does this dream work for the people you love? Does it fit with your current season of life? Is it compatible with your lifestyle?
- Does this dream contribute to the legacy you want to leave behind? Will it last beyond your lifetime?
- How much research is still needed? What kind of field work or test drive might inspire you? What can you do to go deeper?

After the group has identified one of these ongoing considerations, they may offer other observations, suggestions, or encouragement to help you move forward. Remember that this feedback should be positive and helpful—less like *Shark Tank* and more like swimming with dolphins. Each dreamer should listen closely and not interrupt. As the group feedback winds down, you may then ask one question to help you form an action plan.

CLOSE

Close your session by praying for one another's dreams, especially those that seem overwhelming or impossible. Ask God to give you wisdom to discern which big dreams will have the greatest impact on others, fulfill your purpose, and reveal his love to the most people.

Session Two

BETWEEN-SESSIONS PERSONAL STUDY

This week, you may want to review chapters 14–18 in *Dream Big* before engaging in the following between-session activities. Be sure to read the reflection questions after each activity and make a few notes in your guide about the experience. There will be a few minutes for you to share any insights you learned at the start of the next session.

REFLECT: COLLECT YOUR DREAMS

Take a few minutes to reflect on the following questions and record your answers:

Have you ever started to collect something (like books, stamps, or baseball cards) only to become overwhelmed by the number of possible items you could add to your collection? With this in mind, how have you managed your collection of dreams?

Collectors either go for *quantity* (how much they can collect) or for *quality* (only adding rare finds). How does your current list of big dreams compare? Do you have too many items on your list that divide your attention in too many different areas? Explain.

How many dreams do you believe you have successfully achieved or attained in your life? Which ones now seem foolish, selfish, or immature? Which ones have had the greatest impact on the way you evaluate new dreams?

What are some dreams you have abandoned or given up? What has caused you to let go of them? Which of these lost dreams still resonates with your ambitions? Why?

Which dreams do you have that most stir your heart and cause you to feel a powerful sense of urgency? What next step can you take to pursue those dreams?

READ: **GO BIG!**

Read the following passage found in Matthew 25:14–30:

Again, [the kingdom of heaven] will be like a man going on a journey, who called his servants and entrusted his wealth to them. To one he gave five bags of gold, to another two bags, and to another one bag, each according to his ability. Then he went on his journey. The man who had received five bags of gold went at once and put his money to work and gained five bags more. So also, the one with two bags of gold gained two more. But the man who had received one bag went off, dug a hole in the ground and hid his master's money.

After a long time the master of those servants returned and settled accounts with them. The man who had received five bags of gold brought the other five. "Master," he said, "you entrusted me with five bags of gold. See, I have gained five more."

His master replied, "Well done, good and faithful servant! You have been faithful with a few things; I will put you in charge of many things. Come and share your master's happiness!"

The man with two bags of gold also came. "Master," he said, "you entrusted me with two bags of gold; see, I have gained two more." His master replied, "Well done, good and faithful servant! You have been faithful with a few things; I will put you in charge of many things. Come and share your master's happiness!"

Then the man who had received one bag of gold came. "Master," he said, "I knew that you are a hard man, harvesting where you have not sown and gathering where you have

*not scattered seed. So I was afraid and went out and hid your
gold in the ground. See, here is what belongs to you."*

*His master replied, "You wicked, lazy servant! So you
knew that I harvest where I have not sown and gather where
I have not scattered seed? Well then, you should have put my
money on deposit with the bankers, so that when I returned
I would have received it back with interest.*

*"So take the bag of gold from him and give it to the one
who has ten bags. For whoever has will be given more, and
they will have an abundance. Whoever does not have, even
what they have will be taken from them. And throw that
worthless servant outside, into the darkness, where there will
be weeping and gnashing of teeth."*

At first glance, this parable is a simple story about taking
risks. Just like servant #1 and #2, we should take what we've
been given and invest it for the greatest return. But the truth
is that most of us relate more to servant #3, who blew it by
literally burying his master's treasure in the ground. As much
as we might *want* to identify with the two wise investors, most
of us know the kind of fear that motivates servant #3. He's
the person anticipating the future and trying to bypass what
he foresees as likely the most stressful route. He's trying to
avoid any problems that might arise if he lost what he was
entrusted to keep while the boss was traveling.

Knowing that his boss is hard to please, servant #3 makes
it his priority to do whatever it takes to please his demanding
master. He reasons that if he invests the treasure he's been
given and happens to lose it . . . well, his boss would be really
angry and disappointed. Ironically, this status-quo strategy
he chooses sets off the very kind of fireworks the poor guy

was hoping to avoid. His boss is furious, because he risked absolutely nothing!

The implication is that the master would not have been upset if servant #3 had at least *tried* to invest the money and made more out of what he'd been given. Consequently, rather than getting a warm pat on the back like servants #1 and #2, our poor servant gets kicked to the curb. If these consequences for playing it safe seem harsh, it's perhaps because this is exactly the point that Jesus is trying to make. Every investor wants to make the most on a return, but the biggest returns usually result from the greatest risks.

When we talk ourselves out of dreaming big, we're radically reducing our return. When we look ahead and try to fearfully forecast the worst possible outcome, we're second-guessing (or third-servant guessing) our dream and, more importantly, God's ability to bring our ambitions to life. When it comes to our dreams, God really wants us to go big!

When have you played it safe with an opportunity instead of taking a risk to pursue your ambitions? What happened? What did you learn from the experience?

When have you taken a leap of faith and risked what you had to maximize the investment? How did this compare to playing it safe? What made the difference?

How would you describe the master in this parable? Do you think the first two servants perceived their boss to be as demanding as the third servant? Why or why not? How does your view of God influence your willingness to risk what he has entrusted to you?

What treasure are you currently stewarding that needs to be invested in order to pursue your big dreams? What's been holding you back from taking this risk? What do you believe God wants you to do with it?

ACT: TAKE A FIELD TRIP

Artists, writers, inventors, and entrepreneurs will often schedule an appointment to visit a gallery, bookstore, museum, or existing business in order to find new inspiration. These trips can help them get better acquainted with a particular idea, field of study, or industry, or they can help them to explore a new theory, innovation, or possibility.

This week, choose one of your big dreams—ideally the one you feel strongest about pursuing—and take a field trip. Think about the kinds of places that would help you to best learn about different facets of this dream. You might choose to tour a factory, visit an aquarium, explore a nature preserve, volunteer at a non-profit, experience a new restaurant, browse in a small business, create at a craft center, listen to a concert, observe a town council meeting, or organize a community service project. The sky is the limit!

After you've spent some time reflecting, praying, and thinking about some possible locations, come up with a plan. Use the prompts provided below to get specific about where you will go and what you will accomplish while you are there. If possible, give yourself a margin of time to allow for tangents, spontaneous conversations with experts you encounter on your field trip, and inspired note-taking. Your trip will be what you make it, so try to have fun and enjoy the time focusing solely on your budding ambition.

My field trip will be on _____ (day/date) at _____ (time). I will be going to _____ (place) in order to experience _____

_____

(your goals, hopes, expectations). If possible, I would love to talk with _____

_____

(experts, leaders, participants, other dreamers). Some questions that I have are:

_____

_____

_____

_____

_____

_____

_____

I plan to spend at least _____ (amount of time) there learning and experiencing more about _____

_____

_____ (your big dream).

After you have taken your field trip, answer the following questions and think about what you would like to share with your group at the next session.

How did you feel about completing this activity? What felt scary, uncertain, or stressful about it? What felt exciting, hopeful, or inspiring?

What did your trip reveal about your dream that surprised you? How did your experience change or alter the way you feel about this dream?

What do you feel is the next action step to take to bring your dream to life?

For Next Week: Use the space below to write any other key insights or questions from your personal study that you want to discuss at the next group meeting. In preparation for next week, review chapters 19–24 in *Dream Big*.

CLEAR THE PATH

Clearing the path means identifying limiting beliefs
and then moving them aside so you can get at those
beautiful big ambitions that God has for you.

BOB GOFF

WELCOME

When we start to engage in the process of allowing ourselves
to dream big, we often run up against the brick wall of our
limiting beliefs. These are the things we've been told and have
chosen to believe about ourselves based on past experiences,
others' warnings, and our worst fears. We cling to these
assumptions as fact and drag them along with us throughout life. Yet many of these limitations are self-imposed. We
believe what our parents, teachers, coaches, and others have
said about us at a particular place and time. We set those
beliefs in stone, when actually they should be more like sand-
castles that have long since washed away.

As we begin to look at the reasons why we think we can't
pursue our dreams, we will discover new paths through
places that we previously assumed were impassable. In this

respect, other people are usually more willing to help us than we might believe. In fact, their big dreams can intersect with our own to create beautiful bridges that unite what once appeared to be separate and unique ambitions. We can share our needs and our resources and work with others to achieve what we could never create alone.

Clearing the path to make room for our big dreams also requires us to face down our fears and take some leaps of faith. We will have to get out of our comfort zones—and also likely have to experience discomfort, inconvenience, frustration, and disappointment. In other words, we will have to pay a price and make some hard choices. But if we've cleared a path by challenging old beliefs and removing false assumptions, we will have more than enough room to blaze a trail and see our big dreams come to life.

SHARE

To get things started for this third session, discuss the following questions:

- One thing that distracts me the most on any given day is _____
_____
_____.

- One thing that stood out to me in my between-sessions studies that I would like to share with the group is _____
_____.

READ

Invite someone to read aloud the following passage. Listen for new insights as you hear the verses being read and then discuss the questions that follow.

> *As Jesus and his disciples were on their way, he came to a village where a woman named Martha opened her home to him. She had a sister called Mary, who sat at the Lord's feet listening to what he said. But Martha was distracted by all the preparations that had to be made. She came to him and asked, "Lord, don't you care that my sister has left me to do the work by myself? Tell her to help me!"*
>
> *"Martha, Martha," the Lord answered, "you are worried and upset about many things, but few things are needed—or indeed only one. Mary has chosen what is better, and it will not be taken away from her"* (Luke 10:38–42).

Who do you identify with the most in this scene—Mary or Martha? Why?

When have you resented others for not helping you attend to details that had to be done? How did you feel about what was expected of you compared to what you expected of them?

WATCH

Play the video segment for session three. As you watch, use the following outline to record any questions you have or points that stand out to you.

In order to pursue the ambitions that God has for you, it is necessary to clear the path and set aside any long-held, limiting beliefs.

In order to make headway toward your big dreams, you must also be willing to move out of your comfort zone and confront your fears with active faith.

The fastest way to move toward your ambitions is often through other people and their ambitions. When you look for ways to serve others, you will discover new opportunities to bring your dreams—as well as their dreams—to life.

Jesus doesn't want you to play it *safe*. He wants you to be bold and brave as you live out your purpose and fulfill the big dreams that he has for you.

If you know *who you are*, *where you are*, and *what you want*, you will be more willing to take bold risks and giant leaps of faith.

You won't clear the path to pursuing your big dreams all at once. So take it step by step and work toward gradual progress. Go Grand Canyon-deep on your ambitions!

DISCUSS

Take a few minutes to discuss what you just watched and explore these concepts with your group.

1. What are some limiting beliefs that have held you back from taking risks in pursuit of your dreams? Where did these beliefs come from? How have they influenced the decisions you have made in pursuit of your ambitions?

2. When have assumptions about how others would respond to a risk you wanted to take prevented you from taking action? What was the basis for your assumptions?

3. What are the biggest distractions cluttering up your time, energy, and attention each day? What impact do these distractions have on bringing your dreams to life?

4. How does remembering Jesus' example in the Bible of serving others help you to prioritize your pursuit of your God-given dreams?

5. When was the last time you rearranged your schedule or turned down a request in order to keep your dream-path clear?

6. Who are the people currently encouraging, supporting, and fueling the pursuit of your dreams? How are you also helping them fulfill their ambitions?

DREAM BIG

(For this activity, you will need a sheet of paper and a pen or pencil.)

It's easy to fall into the trap of making assumptions about yourself and believing that you don't possess the skill, time, talent, intelligence, finances, or other resources that your dream would require for you to pursue. Yet many of these barriers to your big dreams will actually prove to be rather flimsy once you recognize the limiting beliefs that are holding you back. With this in mind, make three vertical columns on your sheet of paper. Put "obstacle" at the top of the first column, "belief" above the second, and "truth" for the third so it looks something like this:

Obstacle	Belief	Truth
1)		
2)		
3)		

Spend a few minutes listing at least three obstacles to pursuing one of your current dreams, followed by the belief supporting your view of that obstacle. (Leave the third column blank for now.) For example, you might list "not enough time" as an obstacle to actualizing your ambitions followed by the belief, "I need at least four hours a day to act on my dream."

After everyone in the group has come up with three pairs of obstacles/beliefs, swap papers with the person on your left. Now fill in the "truth" column on that person's paper. You can respond with a comment, question, observation, or other reflection of what you see that is true about each listed obstacle/belief. For example, if you wrote down "not enough time" as an obstacle, your partner might respond, "Are you sure you need four hours every day? If so, how can you find some time in your schedule?"

Keep the comments and questions as positive and constructive as possible. Remember, the goal is to help each other see your dream detainers and limiting beliefs more clearly and objectively. Once you've both finished providing "truth," return your papers and compare notes. Talk about what you see in each other's barriers and beliefs that might be worth considering from other viewpoints. If certain obstacles and beliefs do hold up, think about how Jesus' example or the wisdom from the Bible might help determine the next step.

CLOSE

Close your meeting by praying that God would clear the paths in each of your lives, helping you remove distractions and limiting beliefs. Ask that he would give you the courage to move beyond comfort and take the required risks to expand the impact your ambitions can have.

BETWEEN-SESSIONS PERSONAL STUDY

This week, you may want to review chapters 19–24 in *Dream Big* before engaging in the following between-session activities. Be sure to read the reflection questions after each activity and make a few notes in your guide about the experience. There will be a few minutes for you to share any insights you learned at the start of the next session.

REFLECT: IDENTIFY LIMITING BELIEFS

Take a few minutes to reflect on the following questions and record your answers:

What limiting beliefs did you receive in your childhood? These might be messages about your talent, skill level, intelligence, body, size, appearance, gender, or ethnicity. How was this message imparted? How does this limiting belief affect you presently?

What beliefs and assumptions were part of your family culture growing up? These might be about what was considered rude or polite, bad or good, dangerous or safe. How have these family cultural beliefs shaped some of the big decisions in your life?

What's one thing you would change about yourself if you could? Why? What underlying assumption or belief do you hold that compels you to want to change some aspect of yourself? What does it mean to accept, love, and value this part of who you are?

What coping strategies did you learn growing up? How have these helped you make it through those years and into adulthood? How do they continue to serve you now?

Do you agree that if you want to say *yes* to something big, you will have to say *no* to something small? Why or why not? What are some of the small things that you currently need to let go of or no longer continue doing?

READ: PLANT CAREFULLY

Read the following passage found in Matthew 13:1–9:

That same day Jesus went out of the house and sat by the lake. Such large crowds gathered around him that he got into a boat and sat in it, while all the people stood on the shore. Then he told them many things in parables, saying: "A farmer went out to sow his seed. As he was scattering the seed, some fell along the path, and the birds came and ate it up. Some fell on rocky places, where it did not have much soil. It sprang up quickly, because the soil was shallow. But when the sun came up, the plants were scorched, and they withered because they had no root. Other seed fell among thorns, which grew up and choked the plants. Still other seed fell on good soil, where it produced a crop—a hundred, sixty or thirty times what was sown. Whoever has ears, let them hear."

You have probably heard the saying that you "reap what you sow." This concept is not only an old adage but also a truth that is reinforced throughout the Bible (see, for example, Galatians 6:7, John 4:37, and Psalm 126:5). Often, the saying has a negative implication—make sure you sow the right seeds, because you will reap the consequences. But the principle also applies to your dreams. If you want to reap big dreams—the ones that will benefit others and endure beyond your lifetime—you must sow the seeds for those big dreams!

The problem is that often we are like the farmer in Jesus' parable who just scattered seeds everywhere he went. Some of the seed fell along the path as he was walking. Some landed on rocky ground without enough soil to take root. Some dropped into thorn bushes. Each of these sowing spots couldn't support the plant that wanted to take root, sprout, and bear fruit. So, the birds gobbled the seeds on the path, the sun withered the seedlings without deep roots, and the thorns choked out the others.

Fortunately, some of the farmer's seeds did land in good soil, where it produced an incredible harvest—thirty-fold, sixty-fold, and a hundred-fold. As big dreamers, we must consider where we plant our seeds. Our resources of time, energy, health, and money can only go so far. No matter how healthy, wealthy, and wise we may be, our time in this life is finite.

We have to pay attention to where our seed lands if we want to bear fruit—both spiritually and physically—that maximizes our impact. This means making sure we spill as few seeds as possible on our journey, avoiding shallow soil on rocky ground, and planting beyond those pesky thorn bushes. It means focusing on planting in the most fertile soil available so we can yield fruit that exceeds our expectations.

When have you felt like you were scattering the seeds of your resources in non-fruitful directions? When did you realize your efforts were not producing worthwhile results? How did you adjust or change your planting?

Where do you need to stop planting in order to maximize your resources in ways that actualize your dreams? In other words, what small things do you need to say *no* to in order to keep saying *yes* to your God-given ambitions?

What (or who) are the hungry birds, withering sun, and thorny bushes distracting, detaining, and diverting your seeds? How can you overcome them or at least minimize the damage done to your time, talent, and treasure?

When have you seen your efforts explode with good things beyond what you imagined? How has God used your big-dream seeds to produce fruit in the lives of others? Where does he want you to plant right now?

ACT: **TAKE INVENTORY**

In order to plant in good soil and maximize the harvest, farmers clear the field of weeds, rocks, bushes, and debris. They also turn the soil to keep it fertile with the best nutrients. As we have seen, we have to do the same with the seeds of our big dreams if we want to realize a lasting harvest.

Clearing the path, like so much about pursuing big dreams, can be easy to identify and describe but hard to act on. It's not easy to turn down others or to let go of things you've been holding a while. It's tough to change limiting beliefs that have been instilled since childhood. Distractions and interruptions will likely always be nipping at your heels.

But this provides all the more reason to be dedicated and vigilant about your focus. If you want to dream big, you must do some personal clarifying and cleaning in order to stay on track. One way to do this is by taking inventory on a regular basis. Look at what's working, what's not working, what you can change, and what you have to accept for now. Make changes in how you spend your time and resources. Create new habits that support your big dreams.

While you can self-assess in many different ways, check in with where you are and how you can clear the path to your dreams by identifying items in the following categories:

LIMITING BELIEFS TO RELEASE

TIME WASTERS TO OVERCOME

DISTRACTIONS TO ELIMINATE

IMPROVEMENTS TO MAKE

PEOPLE TO INVOLVE

After creating your inventory, complete the following statements and consider sharing with your group at the next session.

The main action I need to take to clear my dream path is _____

_____

_____

because _____

_____ .

When I think of clearing my path and focusing more intently on my big dreams, I feel _____

_____ .

I probably feel this way in part because _____

_____ .

The limiting belief I've been holding that continues to get in my way is _____
_____ .

However, the truth I must remember is that _____
_____ .

For Next Week: Use the space below to write any key insights or questions from your personal study that you want to discuss at the next group meeting. In preparation for next week, review chapters 25–29 in *Dream Big.*

PUSH THROUGH
SETBACKS

On your journey to your big dream,
you're going to fall out of the boat once or twice.

BOB GOFF

WELCOME

We will all face setbacks as we pursue our dreams. Whether we call them mistakes, failures, bad decisions, or just poor judgment, they will leave us feeling sad, angry, frustrated, and confused. These are the times when we may be tempted to abandon our dreams, distance ourselves from God, and chase after pleasurable distractions. But these are the times when we must push through and realize God is with us in the midst of our disappointments.

Setbacks often blindside us, compounding the blow by making us feel unprepared, foolish, or ashamed for what we didn't see coming. The shame can linger and make us reluctant to keep risking or taking leaps of faith in pursuit of our ambitions. What if we fail again? What will other people think? How can we try again after this happened . . . yet again? What am I supposed to learn from this thing that makes no sense?

There are no easy answers, but dealing with setbacks along the trail we're blazing requires patience. We often have to live with the tension of not knowing what purpose a setback serves or how God will use it to further our dreams. We have to be willing to wait despite the fact we want to charge ahead—either in the opposite direction as we run away or toward the possibility of encountering the same setback again.

Time and experience will help us persevere, along with gaining wisdom from the scars we bear. We find new ways to go through, around, or beyond what once seemed insurmountable. We develop abilities, hone skills, and grow stronger as we survive each setback and realize that God hasn't given up on us or left us on our own. He is with us always and gives us power, courage, and tenacity to push through setbacks and fulfill our big dreams.

SHARE

To get things going for this fourth session, discuss the following questions:

- The last time I experienced a setback was _____ _____. How I handled this was to _____.

- One thing that stood out to me in my between-sessions studies that I would like to share with the group is _____.

READ

Invite someone to read aloud the following passage. Listen for new insights as you hear the verses being read and then discuss the questions that follow.

Immediately Jesus made the disciples get into the boat and go on ahead of him to the other side, while he dismissed the crowd. After he had dismissed them, he went up on a mountainside by himself to pray. Later that night, he was there alone, and the boat was already a considerable distance from land, buffeted by the waves because the wind was against it.

Shortly before dawn Jesus went out to them, walking on the lake. When the disciples saw him walking on the lake, they were terrified. "It's a ghost," they said, and cried out in fear.

But Jesus immediately said to them: "Take courage! It is I. Don't be afraid."

"Lord, if it's you," Peter replied, "tell me to come to you on the water."

"Come," he said.

Then Peter got down out of the boat, walked on the water and came toward Jesus. But when he saw the wind, he was afraid and, beginning to sink, cried out, "Lord, save me!"

Immediately Jesus reached out his hand and caught him. "You of little faith," he said, "why did you doubt?"

And when they climbed into the boat, the wind died down. Then those who were in the boat worshiped him, saying, "Truly you are the Son of God" (Matthew 14:22–33).

Why do you think Peter chose this particular test—walking on water—to verify the person he and the disciples saw in the storm was really Jesus?

How did Peter's senses—seeing the waves and feeling himself sink—undermine the miracle of walking on water toward Christ? How do our senses sometimes make it hard to stay focused on Jesus and experience his miraculous power?

WATCH

Play the video segment for session four. As you watch, use the following outline to record any questions you have or points that stand out to you.

We all face difficulties. It's what we do with those difficulties that shapes our faith and how we pursue our big dreams.

God doesn't allow setbacks so we will become desperate but to remind us that he is with us in them. Often the challenge is having the presence of mind to know that he is still with us, no matter how great the setback.

God will burn down whatever it takes to get the truth of our lives to the forefront—despite how painful it may be for us in the moment.

Instead of hiding the scars of our setbacks and failures, we can use them as reminders of where we've been and where we're going—toward our big dreams.

Enduring setbacks requires a lot of patience. When there is something blocking our progress we shouldn't *bail out* but *figure out* what the problem is and how to change our approach.

Staying awake to our ambitions can be tough in the midst of setbacks. But we have to keep the faith and continue to look for opportunities to take risks toward our big dreams.

DISCUSS

Take a few minutes to discuss what you just watched and explore these concepts with your group.

1. How can setbacks derail you from pursuing your dreams? What things can keep you from persevering? Why is it hard to keep your faith strong during these times?

2. How can you choose to keep from sinking, like Peter, when you're "walking on water" during life's storms? What are some ways that you have dealt with doubts, uncertainty, and fear without succumbing to them?

3. When have you seen God redeem a previous setback into something that moved you closer to your dreams? How does this affect the way you view current challenges?

4. What is a setback you've faced that caused you to find a different path, an innovative solution, or a fresh perspective? Why is creativity so important to the process of pushing through setbacks?

5. What helps you practice patience in the midst of long waits, disappointing news, or unexpected losses? When have you seen your patience rewarded in some way?

DREAM

Setbacks can haunt you and leave you with battle scars. One of the best ways to learn from them is to share them with others in a safe environment of mutual trust, respect, and support. By this time, you and your group members have gotten to know one another and to encourage each other's big dreams. So, as you close—and if you are comfortable in doing so—share one setback that continues to impact your life, in either negative or positive ways. Focus on a setback that currently blocks your pursuit of the big dreams you've been exploring in this study.

Don't share anything you don't want to share, but do risk being vulnerable with the group. Next, after you and your fellow group members have had the chance to share a specific setback, echo back what you have heard or ask clarifying questions. Avoid the temptation to offer solutions, fix problems, or counsel with clichés. Instead, simply let the activity of sharing and listening, of being heard and knowing you're not alone, reveal whatever emerges. Let God work through this simple yet powerful act of community.

Again, don't feel pressed to participate, but the benefits to the group will be greater if everyone joins in the conversation. Remember to listen carefully and to respect the confidentiality of the group. What is shared during this time should stay in the group.

CLOSE

Spend a few moments praying silently together before praying aloud. Ask God to help you push through setbacks and trust him when you can't see where you're going and what good can come from the situations that you are facing. Pray for one another and for any challenges that are currently in your lives. Thank God for each other and how you can support and encourage one another through this group.

BETWEEN-SESSIONS PERSONAL STUDY

This week, you may want to review chapters 25–29 in *Dream Big* before engaging in the following between-session activities. Be sure to read the reflection questions after each activity and make a few notes in your guide about the experience. There will be a few minutes for you to share any insights you learned at the start of the next session.

REFLECT: **FAIL FORWARD**

Take a few minutes to reflect on the following questions and record your answers:

> How has your pride gotten in the way of pushing through some of the setbacks you've faced? When have you focused more on how you looked in a situation than on actually being prepared to deal with it?

Can you relate to choosing a Harley only to discover you really need to ride a Vespa in order to push through a setback? What did your Vespa-choice look like? In other words, how did you use your resourcefulness to overcome the obstacle in your way?

Have you ever blamed God for a setback when really your performance (or lack of preparation) caused the problem? Do you agree it's easier to blame God or others rather than take responsibility to bring your ambitions to life? Why or why not?

What is one of the epic failures in your life? How did it devastate you at the time? What consequences continue to linger from it? What has it shown you about yourself that you're still here and pursuing the big dreams that God has given you?

What battle scars do you live with that remind you of past setbacks? How can they give you present strength and future hope rather than be a souvenir of past pain?

When has your tenacity and perseverance paid off in pursuit of a goal? What role did your faith play in reaching this goal? How can you apply the same ingredients as you move toward bringing your ambitions to life?

READ: **WAIT PATIENTLY**

Read the following passage found in Psalm 40:1–5:

> I waited patiently for the LORD;
>   he turned to me and heard my cry.
> He lifted me out of the slimy pit,
>   out of the mud and mire;
> he set my feet on a rock
>   and gave me a firm place to stand.
> He put a new song in my mouth,
>   a hymn of praise to our God.
> Many will see and fear the LORD
>   and put their trust in him.

Blessed is the one
who trusts in the LORD,
who does not look to the proud,
to those who turn aside to false gods.
Many, LORD *my God,*
are the wonders you have done,
the things you planned for us.
None can compare with you;
were I to speak and tell of your deeds,
they would be too many to declare.

Many of the psalms in the Bible, including this one, were written by a shepherd boy from Bethlehem named David who would later become the king of Israel. He was the youngest in his family and almost forgotten when Samuel, God's prophet, came looking for him. When Samuel saw David—who had just come in from tending his sheep—he did a double-take and asked God if he really was to be the next king. God made it clear that he looks at the heart, not on outward appearances. So Samuel anointed the teenager as God's chosen sovereign to rule over his people.

The only problem was that a man named Saul was currently on the throne. David would have to wait a while—probably fifteen years—before becoming king. From the moment of his anointing, David experienced one setback after another. His life was messy at times. But through every setback, heartbreak, and letdown, he remained committed to God. In fact, in spite of the messiness, David was called God's friend and a man after the Lord's own heart.

Many of David's psalms reflect this up-and-down struggle. But as we see in this psalm, he knew what it meant to have to wait on God to pull him up out of the muddy pit. He knew that God would not abandon him or leave him to be swallowed by his frustrations, disappointments, fears, and doubts. He knew that God would help him to get back on his feet.

What psalms, verses, or passages of Scripture have given you strength, courage, hope, and inspiration in the midst of life's setbacks?

What other books, songs, poetry, or works of art have inspired you to persevere? How do they express your feelings as you push through adversity toward your dreams?

Can you think of a situation you have been in—such as a white-water rapids ride or treacherous hike—that illustrates what it's like to survive a dangerous setback?

If you were going to write a poem or psalm about how God has been present with you during hard times and setbacks, what images and descriptions would you use?

ACT: **REKINDLE THE FIRE**

It's painful to revisit places where you encountered painful setbacks and dream-wounding disappointments. Like visiting a cemetery or memorial, such a return may seem at best bittersweet as you reflect on what occurred there, how you felt at the time, and what the consequences were. But such return visits can also be liberating in the way they help you see how you have overcome those obstacles and made it to this point in your life.

This week, choose a "setback site" that's within your ability to visit. This could be the home where you grew up, an office building where you worked, a hospital where you were treated, a school you attended, or a restaurant where you were blindsided by a break-up. During your visit, spend a few minutes reflecting, praying, or journaling about what you experienced there and how you have since survived, matured, and grown stronger. Celebrate the fact you pushed through and did not allow the setback to kill your spirit.

After your visit—or perhaps as part of it—thank God for being with you through this painful time of your life. Also, find a way to honor your willingness to persevere and not give up on your dreams. You might leave flowers there, volunteer for an hour or two, bring a small gift for someone residing or working there, or enjoy a coffee as you sit and pray and reflect. If you feel inspired, you could even talk with someone there and share the purpose of your visit.

The key is to reframe the way you view this setback and this place you have associated with it. Turn it into an altar of thanksgiving rather than a shame-filled site of regret. After your visit, take a few minutes to think about your experience and how it felt. Answer the following questions and write down anything you want to share with the group at your final session.

Why did you choose the place you visited? When was the last time you were there? How did you feel when you arrived at this site?

What is the biggest change you've experienced since this setback occurred?

How did you celebrate or commemorate your visit—flowers, a prayer, or something else? How did you feel as you left this place this time?

For Next Week: Use the space below to write any key insights or questions from your personal study that you want to discuss at the next group meeting. In preparation for next week, review chapters 30–31 in *Dream Big*.

LAND THE PLANE

Stop talking about what you want to do someday
and just start—do something!

BOB GOFF

WELCOME

Follow-through can be hard for all of us. But there comes a point in any endeavor when you've done all the research, all the envisioning, and all the path-clearing and just need to move forward. This study has attempted to help you answer life's three big questions: *Who are you? Where are you? What do you want?* Now it's time to act on your answers.

It can be tempting to continue doing these activities that keep you flying high with excitement and fresh adrenaline. Planning, imagining, talking, speculating, searching, and finding—they're all vital parts of the process. Eventually, however, you have to make your ambitions concrete. You have to *land that plane* of ideas so that its passengers can take action.

You might think landing a plane is simple, but there is actually an interval right before touchdown when it feels as if you're floating above the runway. As the pilot decelerates or cuts the engine, the plane hovers ten to fifteen feet in the air before its wheels hit the ground. This phenomenon is called "ground effect," as the wind traveling past the underside of the wings pushes against the ground, creating a gentle—or not so gentle—lift from below.

Putting your dreams in action often feels like experiencing ground effect. You're hovering along when suddenly—*bam!*—you hit the ground. The impact is jarring, and the contents of your overhead compartments definitely may have shifted! In other words, getting started with real steps that force you to do something won't be easy. But it doesn't have to be smooth or perfect. It only has to get you on the road to taking action!

SHARE

To begin this final session, discuss the following questions:

- A key idea that stands out from this study is _____
  _____ .

- One thing that stood out to me in my between-sessions studies that I would like to share with the group is _____ .

READ

Invite someone to read aloud the following passage. Listen for new insights as you hear the verses being read and then discuss the questions that follow.

When the Son of Man comes in his glory, and all the angels with him, he will sit on his glorious throne. All the nations will be gathered before him, and he will separate the people one from another as a shepherd separates the sheep from the goats. He will put the sheep on his right and the goats on his left.

Then the King will say to those on his right, "Come, you who are blessed by my Father; take your inheritance, the kingdom prepared for you since the creation of the world. For I was hungry and you gave me something to eat, I was thirsty and you gave me something to drink, I was a stranger and you invited me in, I needed clothes and you clothed me, I was sick and you looked after me, I was in prison and you came to visit me."

Then the righteous will answer him, "Lord, when did we see you hungry and feed you, or thirsty and give you something to drink? When did we see you a stranger and invite you in, or needing clothes and clothe you? When did we see you sick or in prison and go to visit you?"

The King will reply, "Truly I tell you, whatever you did for one of the least of these brothers and sisters of mine, you did for me."

Then he will say to those on his left, "Depart from me, you who are cursed, into the eternal fire prepared for the devil and his angels. For I was hungry and you gave me nothing to eat, I was thirsty and you gave me nothing to drink, I was a stranger and you did not invite me in, I needed clothes and you did not clothe me, I was sick and in prison and you did not look after me."

They also will answer, "Lord, when did we see you hungry or thirsty or a stranger or needing clothes or sick or in prison, and did not help you?"

He will reply, "Truly I tell you, whatever you did not do for one of the least of these, you did not do for me" (Matthew 25:31–45).

What stands out to you about the criteria used here to separate the sheep from the goats? How does meeting the physical needs of others demonstrate God's love?

Why do you suppose feeding hungry people, showing hospitality to outsiders, and visiting those who are sick or in prison pleases God?

WATCH

Play the video segment for session five. As you watch, use the following outline to record any questions you have or points that stand out to you.

Landing the plane of your dreams and getting your feet on the ground won't be easy. It's going to take a load of authenticity to get there. It's going to take being vulnerable—hopefully with the people who are surrounding you in this small group.

God wants to do something amazing through you. It's going to look a lot like landing the plane—moving from the bleachers to the field—as you choose to go after your ambitions.

Some of the things you think are keeping you away from your ambition aren't the real things that are keeping you away. You need to figure out the real obstacles and then make moves to remove them.

Landing the plane involves quitting a couple of things so you can prioritize your dreams. It's going Grand Canyon with some routines and practices you do in your life weekly

When an ambition looks like it's not working, first *pick where you're going, lean forward into your ambition,* and *fill the window with Jesus.*

Do something to get started. Not everything is going to work out the way you hoped, but you can't let that get in the way of pursuing your beautiful ambition.

DISCUSS

Take a few minutes to discuss what you just watched and explore these concepts with your group.

1. Prior to this group study, how long have you been harboring and nurturing your dreams? How has this study influenced your perspective on your ambitions? What action do you need to take now?

2. What are you most tempted to do to avoid landing your plane? More research? More conversations with others? More planning and preparation?

3. What has prevented you from taking actions on your ambitions up until now? How have they impeded your progress or blocked your path? How have you overcome them?

4. How have your fears—both fear of success as well as fear of failure—colored your willingness to take concrete steps for big-dream activation? How can you acknowledge your fears but still take action and do what needs to be done to get started?

5. Imagine yourself a year from now, reuniting with the group to update them on your progress. What do you want to tell them? Where do you see yourself in relation to your ambitions in twelve months? What do you need to do to make this happen?

DREAM

(For this activity, you will need a sheet of paper and a pen or pencil.)

During the past four sessions, your group has completed an activity related to each big idea for that week. You have shared your ambitions, helped vet each other's dreams, dispelled limiting beliefs and distractions, and celebrated how you have endured and grown from past setbacks. Now, for this final activity, it's time to share your action plan for the next steps you will take to make your dream a reality. It's time to hold one another accountable with encouragement, support, prayers, and shared resources. Do this by completing the following action plan:

ACTION PLAN

In one sentence, my big dream is _____

_____

_____ .

My big dream serves others by _____

_____ .

The primary people who will benefit from my dream are _____

_____ .

The action I'm going to take this week to land my plane is _____

_____

_____ .

The group members I will call after I've completed this step are _____

_____ .

If I haven't called them by _____, then they will call me.

What I need most from the group to take action now is _____

_____ .

After you have completed your action plan, pass it to the person on your right, and then keep passing them along until everyone in the group has shared. Make sure you know who you can call from the group in the following weeks and who will be calling you. Conclude by sharing other ways that you and your fellow group members can continue to support one another as you work to bring your ambitions to life. At the very least, commit to praying for each other as you do the scary, exhilarating action of landing your plane, enacting your action plan, and making your big dream a tangible reality.

CLOSE

Close this last meeting sharing one final big-dream-related request. Thank God for all that you have learned in this study and for the beautiful and unique dreams that he has given to you. Ask him for the power, courage, wisdom, and perseverance to keep dreaming big as you change the world by showing his love to everyone you meet.

FINAL PERSONAL STUDY

This week, you may want to review chapters 30–31 in *Dream Big* before engaging in this final personal study. Be sure to read the reflection questions after each activity and make a few notes in your guide about the experience. Share with your group leader or group members in the upcoming weeks any key points or insights that stood out to you.

REFLECT: REVIEW WHAT YOU'VE LEARNED

Take a few minutes to reflect on the following questions and record your answers:

Where are you now compared to where you were when you first started this study? How have you changed or grown the most? What is different about your level of commitment to your ambitions and how you will bring them to life?

Which of the sessions made the greatest impact toward activating your big dreams? Why? How did other group members influence, encourage, and support you?

In the past, what opportunities to take action on your dreams have you missed or allowed to pass by? What will prevent you from missing such opportunities again?

What does it look like for you to create your own model as to the way your dream will take shape and come to life?

What would you do differently to get your dream in motion if you had all the resources—time, money, energy, everything—that you wish you had? How does making action conditional on having more or enough prevent you from doing anything?

What will you do today to ensure you take at least one baby step in faith to act on your ambitions? How do you feel as you get ready to land your plane? How do you imagine you will feel tomorrow after completing this action?

READ: **LEAD BY SERVING**

Read the following passage found in Matthew 20:20–28:

Then the mother of Zebedee's sons came to Jesus with her sons and, kneeling down, asked a favor of him.

"What is it you want?" he asked.

She said, "Grant that one of these two sons of mine may sit at your right and the other at your left in your kingdom."

"You don't know what you are asking," Jesus said to them. "Can you drink the cup I am going to drink?"

"We can," they answered.

Jesus said to them, "You will indeed drink from my cup, but to sit at my right or left is not for me to grant. These places belong to those for whom they have been prepared by my Father."

When the ten heard about this, they were indignant with the two brothers. Jesus called them together and said, "You know that the rulers of the Gentiles lord it over them, and their high officials exercise authority over them. Not so with you. Instead, whoever wants to become great among you must be your servant, and whoever wants to be first must be your slave—just as the Son of Man did not come to be served, but to serve, and to give his life as a ransom for many."

As this passage relates, no matter how often you check your ego or practice humility, it's always good to remember *why* you are doing what you are doing. As you take action and realize your dreams, it's only natural to get hung up on yourself in the middle of it. If things go well, you will begin to feel good about yourself—which is good! But once you feel this sense of accomplishment and success, you can be tempted to take credit for achieving your ambitions.

Never allow yourself to be fooled into thinking that you brought your dream alive by yourself or that you can ultimately claim credit. This is because once you become a successful dreamer, you can begin to cling to your ambitions for your identity. You can enjoy being the person who started that thing that does so much good for others. You can see yourself as indispensable to the mission—the same cause that you know is so much bigger than you.

On the other hand, if your actions fail to land, you may also begin to feel that you are solely to blame. You put yourself back in the midst of those old limiting beliefs and think the old assumptions are true after all. You feel defeated when, in truth, you're just getting started. The only way your failure is fatal is if you let it take you out of the game. If one action doesn't work, try something else. Move in a different direction. Trade your Harley for a Vespa!

Whatever you do, don't give up. Remember Jesus' example and the suffering he endured and the price he paid. This is what he pointed out here to his disciples' mom as well as to his followers: *If you want to love the same way I'm here to love, then it will cost you. But the cost is worth it!* So take action. Show the love of Jesus by what you do and how you do it. Remember the hard work you've done, the setbacks you've overcome, and the way you've kept going. Above all, remember how God has helped you and sustained you and been present with you throughout this entire journey. He is not going to stop now—and neither should you!

Which do you think would be a greater struggle for you: if your dream came to life and wildly succeeded or if your efforts failed to activate your ambitions right now?

Which is easier for you to own and accept—your achievements or your setbacks? Why?

What does it look like for you to remain humble and follow Jesus' example as you take action on your dreams?

What does Jesus' brand of servant leadership look like in the context of what you're doing?

ACT: PITCH, PICK, POINT!

When the engine of an aircraft fails and pilots have to do an emergency landing, the procedure they follow can be summed up as "pitch, pick, point." Pilots rehearse these three steps repeatedly so that when they have to rely on them, they know what to do.

Pitch means the pilots aim the plane back down toward the ground. While this may feel counterintuitive, it makes sense because there is nowhere to land safely in the sky! After the pilots pitch the plane forward and downward, the next step is to *pick* a spot where the plane can land as safely as possible—in a field, empty highway, vacant parking lot, or wherever. The pilots then *point* at that chosen spot and bring the plane down as smoothly as possible.

This same system works for "landing your plane" and making your dreams a reality. Here are the ways you can apply the pitch-pick-point system to your ambitions.

PITCH

Who is one person you want to have cheering you on as you take this first big step? Maybe it's a family member, close friend, boss, mentor, pastor, or teacher. Ideally, the person should have some connection to the goal of your dream work, so choose someone who represents something significant about the focus of your ambitions. Let the person symbolize the general direction of your dream actions—your *pitch* as you aim your plane down and prepare to land.

Contact this person and let him or her know what you're doing as simply and directly as possible. Don't ask for money, or sponsorship, or anything other than the person's prayers and shared interest. After you reach out, thank the person for his or her enthusiasm and willingness to cheer you on. Let the person know that if there is no objection, you would like to provide updates on the ongoing growth of your dream as you take more actions to make it happen.

PICK

Pull up the dream map that you created back in the "Dream" activity from session one. Reflect for a few moments on why you sketched this map the way you did, what you were thinking, and how you were feeling in terms of the ways this map could represent your journey. Does it still seem generally accurate about the direction you want to go as you take action to activate your ambitions?

Make adjustments, revisions, or additions as necessary. Or create an entirely new map based on what you know now that you didn't know then. Once you're relatively satisfied with your dream map, look at where you are on it and where your dream destination is. What is one step you can take right now, today, to move in that direction? It's time to do it! Tell yourself, "I'm going to do this!" After doing this step, there nothing left but to . . .

POINT

Now that you have your big-dream target in place, it's time to get your plane on the ground. No more delays, distractions, or dilly-dallying! Go and do something—*anything*—that will get you closer to seeing your dream come to life. Enjoy the thrill of knowing you are doing what God has created you to do! Feel the rush of joy that comes from meeting a need for other human beings. Keep walking, one step after another, until you're there. Little by little, you will reach the reality of what it means to dream big!

LEADER'S GUIDE

Thank you for agreeing to lead a small group through this study! What you have chosen to do is valuable and will make a great difference in the lives of others.

Dream Big is a five-session study built around video content and small-group interaction. As the group leader, think of yourself as the host of a dinner party. Your job is to take care of your guests by managing all the behind-the-scenes details so that when everyone arrives, they can just enjoy time together. Your role is *not* to answer all the questions or reteach the content—the video, book, and study guide will do that work—but to guide the experience and create an environment where people can process, question, and reflect on the material.

Make sure everyone in the group has a copy of the study guide and knows they are free to write in it. This will keep everyone on the same page and help the group time run more smoothly. If some members are unable to purchase the guide, arrange it so they can share the resource with other group members. Giving everyone access to the materials will position this study to be as rewarding an experience as possible.

SETTING UP THE GROUP

You will need to determine with your group how long you want to meet each week so that you can plan your time accordingly. Generally, most groups like to meet for either ninety minutes or two hours, so you could use one of the following schedules:

SECTION	90 MINUTES	120 MINUTES
WELCOME (members arrive and get settled)	10 minutes	15 minutes
SHARE (discuss opening questions)	10 minutes	15 minutes
READ (discuss the questions based on the Scripture reading for the week)	10 minutes	15 minutes
WATCH (watch the teaching material)	20 minutes	20 minutes
DISCUSS (discuss the questions you selected)	30 minutes	40 minutes
DREAM / CLOSE (do the closing activity and pray together as a group)	10 minutes	15 minutes

As the group leader, you will want to create an environment that encourages sharing and learning. In this regard, a church sanctuary or formal classroom may not be as ideal as a living room, because those locations can feel formal and less intimate. However, no matter what setting you choose, provide enough comfortable seating for everyone, and, if possible, arrange the seats in a semicircle so everyone can see the video easily. This will make transition between the video and group conversation more efficient and natural.

Also, try to get to the meeting site early so you can greet participants as they arrive. Simple refreshments create a welcoming atmosphere and can be a wonderful addition to a group study evening. Try to take food and pet allergies into account to make your guests as comfortable as possible. You may also want to consider offering childcare to couples with children who want to attend. Finally, be sure your media technology is working properly. Managing these details up front will make the rest of your group experience flow smoothly and provide a welcoming space in which to engage the content of *Dream Big.*

STARTING YOUR GROUP TIME

Once everyone has arrived, it's time to begin the group. Here are some simple tips to make your group time healthy, enjoyable, and effective.

First, begin the meeting with prayer and then remind the group members to put their phones on silent. This is a way to make sure you can all be present with one another and with God. Next, give each person a few minutes to respond to the questions in the "Share" section. You won't need much time in session one, but beginning in session two, people will likely need more time to share their insights from their personal studies. Usually, you won't answer the discussion questions yourself, but you should go first with the "Share" questions, answering briefly and with a reasonable amount of transparency.

At the end of session one, invite the group members to complete the between-sessions personal studies for that week. Explain that you will be providing some time before the video teaching next week for anyone to share insights. Let them know sharing is optional, and it's no problem if they can't get to some of the between-sessions activities some weeks. It will still be beneficial for them to hear from the other participants and learn about what they discovered.

LEADING THE DISCUSSION TIME

Now that the group is engaged, it's time to watch the video and respond with some directed small-group discussion. Encourage the group members to participate, but make sure they know they don't have to do so. As the discussion progresses, you may want to follow up with comments such as, "Tell me more about that," or, "Why did you answer that way?" This will allow the participants to deepen their reflections and invite meaningful sharing.

Note that you have been given multiple questions to use in each session, and you do not have to use them all or even follow them in order. Feel free to pick and choose questions based on either the needs of your group or how the conversation is flowing. Also, don't be afraid of silence. Offering a question and allowing up to thirty seconds of silence is okay. It allows people space to think about how they want to respond and also gives them time to do so.

As group leader, you are the boundary keeper for your group. Do not let anyone (yourself included) dominate the group time. Keep an eye out for group members who might be tempted to "attack" folks they disagree with or try to "fix" those having struggles. These kinds of behaviors can derail a group's momentum, so they need to be steered in a different direction. Model active listening and encourage everyone in your group to do the same. This will make your group time a safe space and create a positive community.

The group discussion time leads to a closing individual activity. During this time, encourage the participants to take just a few minutes to review what they've learned and complete the exercise. This will help them cement the big ideas in their minds as you close the session. Close your time together with prayer as a group.

Thank you again for taking the time to lead your group. You are making a difference in the lives of others as you help them to *dream big* and step into the plans that God has for them.

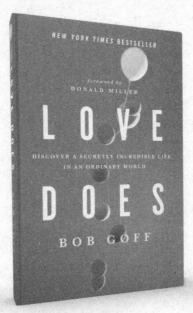

The *Love Does* small group experience is a five-session video Bible study about God's love . . . and the most amazing thing about that love is that it's not just a bunch of rules or stuff we have to agree with. God's love is different. It changes things. It's active. It works. It risks. God's love . . . does. Each session explores a different aspect of God's active love through the stories of Bob Goff.

Available now at your favorite bookstore,
or streaming video on StudyGateway.com.

Streaming
Video

DVD
9781400206292

Study Guide
9781400206278

THOMAS NELSON
Since 1798

ALSO AVAILABLE FROM BOB GOFF

WHAT HAPPENS WHEN WE GIVE AWAY LOVE LIKE WE'RE MADE OF IT?

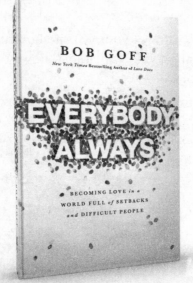

Book
9780718078133

Driven by Bob's trademark storytelling, *Everybody, Always* reveals the lessons Bob learned—often the hard way— about what it means to love without inhibition, insecurity, or restriction. From finding the right friends to discovering the upside of failure, *Everybody, Always* points the way to embodying love by doing the unexpected, the intimidating, the seemingly impossible. Whether losing his shoes while skydiving solo or befriending a Ugandan witch doctor, Bob steps into life with a no-limits embrace of others that is as infectious as it is extraordinarily ordinary. *Everybody, Always* reveals how we can do the same.

In this five-session video Bible study, Bob shares some of the stories from his life that have helped him understand what it truly means to love everybody the way Jesus loved them—without fear, insecurity, or restriction. Following Christ means more than just putting a toe in the water when it comes to loving others. It means grabbing your knees and doing a cannonball! And, as Jesus revealed, it means loving even the difficult ones. *Everybody, Always* will provide practical steps to help you take that journey.

Available now at your favorite bookstore,
or streaming video on StudyGateway.com.

| Streaming Video | DVD 9780310095361 | Study Guide 9780310095330 |

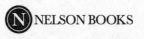

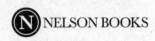